INDIGENOUS BIOGRAPHIES

Madison Hammond

Soccer Star

FOCUS READERS BEACON

by Katrina M. Phillips

www.focusreaders.com

Focus Readers is distributed by North Star Editions:
sales@northstareditions.com | 888-417-0195

Produced for Focus Readers by Red Line Editorial.

Photographs ©: Lindsey Wasson/AP Images, cover, 1; Bryan Byerly/ISI Photos/Getty Images, 4; Rob Gray/ISI Photos/Getty Images, 6; iStockphoto, 8, 13, 29; Shutterstock Images, 11, 14; Brian Westerholt/Sports On Film, 17; Jeff Halstead/Icon Sportswire, 19; Don Ryan/AP Images, 21; Abbie Parr/Getty Images Sport/Getty Images, 22; Ronald Martinez/Getty Images Sport/Getty Images, 24; Ryan Sun/AP Images, 27

Library of Congress Cataloging-in-Publication Data
Names: Phillips, Katrina M., author.
Title: Madison Hammond: soccer star / by Katrina M. Phillips.
Description: Mendota Heights, MN: Focus Readers Beacon, [2026] | Series: Indigenous biographies | Includes bibliographical references and index. | Audience: Grades 2-3
Identifiers: LCCN 2025020307 (print) | LCCN 2025020308 (ebook) | ISBN 9798889985006 (hardcover) | ISBN 9798889986546 paperback | ISBN 9798889985631 (pdf) | ISBN 9798889985327 (ebook)
Subjects: LCSH: Hammond, Madison--Juvenile literature. | Women soccer players--Biography--Juvenile literature. | Indian athletes--Biography--Juvenile literature. | LCGFT: Biographies. | Literature.
Classification: LCC GV942.7.H28 P45 2026 (print) | LCC GV942.7.H28 (ebook) | DDC 796.3340092 [B]--dc23/eng/20250617
LC record available at https://lccn.loc.gov/2025020307
LC ebook record available at https://lccn.loc.gov/2025020308

Printed in the United States of America
Mankato, MN
012026

About the Author

Dr. Katrina M. Phillips (Red Cliff Ojibwe) is a writer, researcher, and history professor. She's written several children's books about Native histories and cultures, including *Indigenous Peoples' Day* and *I Am on Indigenous Land*. She and her husband live in Minnesota with their two sons and their goofy dog.

Table of Contents

OL REIGN
zulily
99
5

CHAPTER 1

Making History

Madison Hammond took the field late in a 2020 match. She was a defender for the Reign. They were facing off against the Utah Royals. Hammond played for only eight minutes.

The Reign are based in the Seattle-Tacoma area in the state of Washington.

Hammond (99) defends a free kick during a 2020 game against the Utah Royals.

After the game, a reporter asked her to do an interview. Hammond was confused. She hadn't played much. She didn't know why anyone would want to interview her.

Then Hammond learned that she'd made history in those eight minutes. She had become the first Native person to play in the National Women's Soccer League (NWSL). She was just 22 years old.

Did You Know?

The NWSL was founded in 2012. The first games were played in the spring of 2013.

CHAPTER 2

Leaving Home

Madison Hammond was born on November 15, 1997, in Phoenix, Arizona. She grew up in the San Felipe Pueblo in New Mexico. Her mother is Navajo and San Felipe Pueblo. Her father is Black.

Albuquerque, New Mexico (pictured), is about 30 miles (48 km) south of the San Felipe Pueblo.

For Madison, being **Indigenous** and Black has shaped many of her life experiences.

Madison started playing soccer when she was five years old. There weren't any girls' teams for kids her age. But she didn't let that stop her. She played on boys' teams instead.

Did You Know?

Madison Hammond is a member of the Fox Clan in the San Felipe Pueblo.

In the United States, millions of children play soccer.

Madison's mother was in the military. Many military families move around a lot. That happened to Madison when she was nine.

She moved to Virginia with her mother and sister. It was hard to be away from her **culture**. She missed the community where she had grown up.

Soccer helped Madison adjust to her new school and her new city. But it wasn't always easy. Some kids teased her for being Native. Other players called her names during games.

Even so, Madison stayed focused on sports. She started playing with

Keres is a Pueblo language. Madison Hammond's Keres name is Shrewaka, which means "magpie." A magpie is a type of bird.

a girls' soccer club. She joined an **elite** team. She first played as an **attacking midfielder**. Later, she started playing as a defender.

A CALL TO CONVERSATION
C2C.WFU.EDU

CHAPTER 3

Finding Her Way

Madison Hammond wanted to keep playing soccer in college. In 2016, she began her first year at Wake Forest University. As a freshman, she earned a starting spot on the soccer team.

Wake Forest University is in Winston-Salem, North Carolina.

Hammond helped the team excel on defense. Wake Forest posted seven shutouts in 2016. The team's defense got even better her next year. Wake Forest gave up less than one goal per game on average.

Hammond still struggled to find her place. In her first two years, she was one of only two players on the team who weren't white. However, Hammond developed into a leader. She became a team captain her senior year.

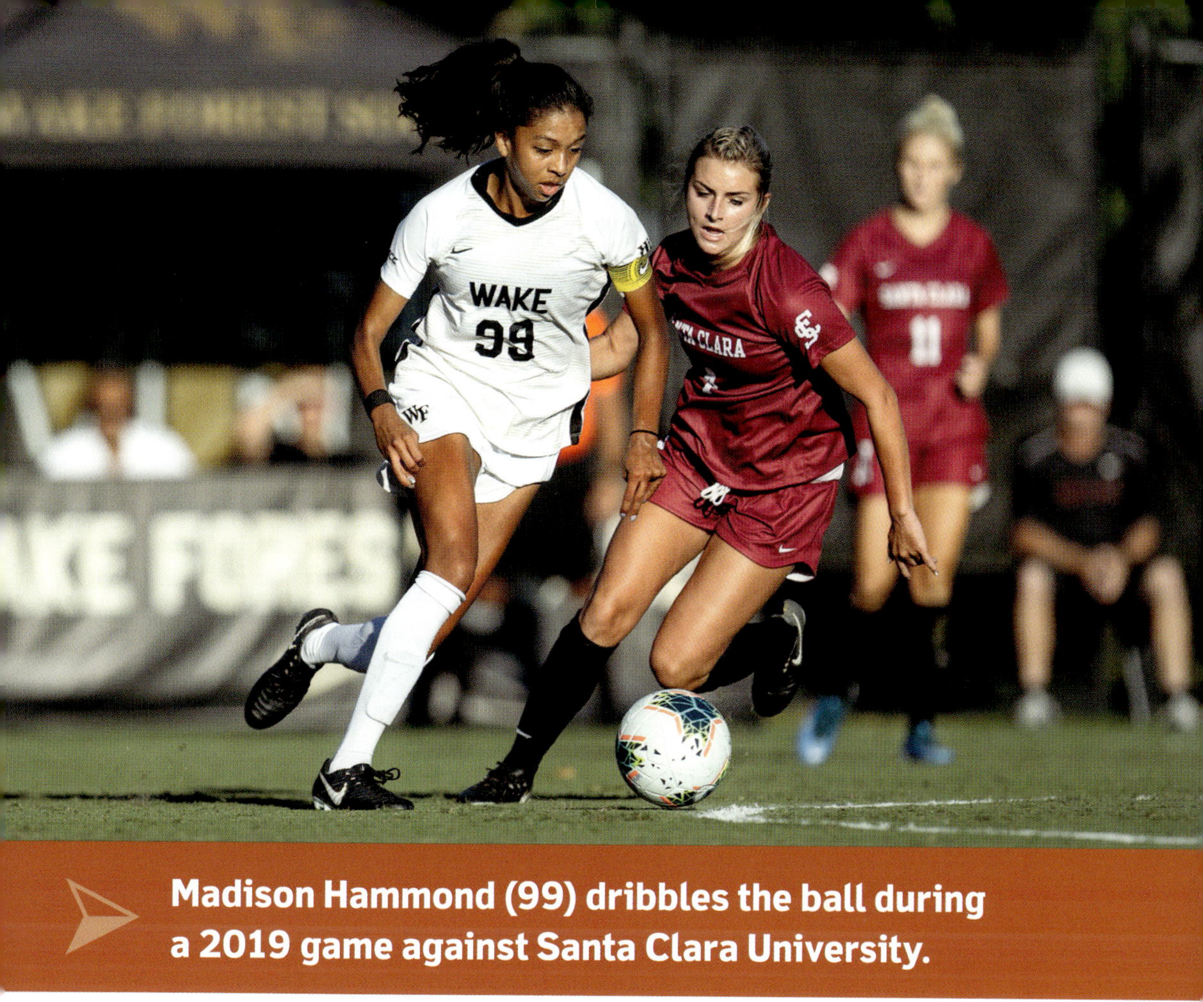

Madison Hammond (99) dribbles the ball during a 2019 game against Santa Clara University.

Like many athletes, Hammond dreamed of playing professional sports. She even finished college early in 2019. That way, she could join a pro team the next year.

In January 2020, the Reign offered Hammond a spot. But she didn't have a **contract** yet. Then COVID-19 hit. The **pandemic** was dangerous. For safety, many professional sports teams canceled their games. Hammond didn't know if she'd ever start her pro career.

Did You Know?

Hammond's uncle is Notah Begay III. He is the first Native person to play in the Professional Golf Association (PGA).

Hammond competes in a 2020 game against the Utah Royals.

Eventually, the Reign let her try out for the team. They gave her a contract in June. Hammond had made it to the NWSL.

TOPIC SPOTLIGHT

Native Athletes

The Nike N7 program began in 2009. This program celebrates the heritage of Native people. It offers sports opportunities for Native kids. Nike also works with Native **designers**. They create collections, including shoes and jerseys. Then, **ambassadors** help promote the collections. Sales support the program's sports opportunities.

Indigenous athletes serve as the ambassadors. In 2021, Madison Hammond became a Nike N7 ambassador. She helped design a sneaker. She included many bright colors. They were based on a **traditional** belt from her godparents.

A Nike worker shows off an early version of an N7 shoe.

BLACK
FUTURE
CO
OP FUND
OL REIGN

CHAPTER 4

Athlete and Activist

Over the years, the NWSL kept adding new teams such as Angel City FC in Los Angeles, California. After playing for the Reign in 2021, Madison Hammond was traded to Angel City in 2022.

Madison Hammond takes part in a 2021 game between the Reign and the Chicago Red Stars.

Hammond fires a kick during a 2023 match between Angel City FC and the Reign.

That year, Angel City played a game in Louisville, Kentucky. Hammond's mother met a Navajo family there. They had driven all the way from Ohio. They had come just to see Hammond. Hammond understood the impact she'd already had. She knew it was important to be a good role model.

Madison Hammond was proud of being the first Native NWSL player. But she didn't want to stop there. So, she kept improving her game. For example, she worked on clearing the ball with her left foot.

Hammond's hard work paid off. In the 2023 season, she earned more playing time than she had in 2022.

She played even more in 2024. Angel City also began playing Hammond at midfield.

Madison Hammond has played soccer all across the United States. But she still goes back to the San Felipe Pueblo every year. May 1 is the San Felipe Pueblo Feast Day.

Did You Know?

Hammond scored her first NWSL goal in 2023. The goal came against her former team, the Reign.

Hammond leaps into a teammate's arms after scoring her first NWSL goal.

It is a 400-year-old tradition. It's very important to the people of the pueblo. It's part of who she is, just like being a professional soccer player.

Focus Questions

Write your answers on a separate piece of paper.

1. Write a letter to a friend about Madison Hammond's career.
2. Would you want to be a professional athlete? Why or why not?
3. Which team did Hammond join in 2022?
    A. Wake Forest
    B. Reign
    C. Angel City FC
4. When did Hammond play in her first professional soccer game?
    A. 2016
    B. 2020
    C. 2024

5. What does **promote** mean in this book?

*Then, ambassadors help **promote** the collections. Sales support the program's sports opportunities.*

- **A.** to bring attention to
- **B.** to get rid of
- **C.** to try out for

6. What does **role model** mean in this book?

*They had come just to see Hammond. Hammond understood the impact she'd already had. She knew it was important to be a good **role model**.*

- **A.** someone who looks for talented players
- **B.** someone who plays defense on a team
- **C.** someone who others look up to as an example

Answer key on page 32.

Glossary

ambassadors
Official representatives of a country or organization.

attacking midfielder
A soccer player who plays in the middle of the field. The player tries to help score goals.

contract
An agreement to pay someone a certain amount of money.

culture
The customs, arts, beliefs, and laws of a group of people.

designers
People who create plans for clothing and accessories.

elite
The best of the best.

Indigenous
Native to a region, or belonging to ancestors who lived in a region before colonists arrived.

pandemic
A disease that spreads quickly around the world.

traditional
Based on ways of doing something that are passed down over many years.

To Learn More

BOOKS

Gish, Ashley. *National Women's Soccer League.* Bellwether Media, 2025.

Goldstein, Margaret J. *Women's Professional Soccer.* Lerner Publications, 2026.

IllumiNative, ed. *My Life: Growing Up Native in America.* MTV Books, 2024.

NOTE TO EDUCATORS

Visit **www.focusreaders.com** to find links and resources related to this title.

Index